FORGING
FREEDOM

A True Story of Heroism during the Holocaust

by **Hudson Talbott**

G. P. Putnam's Sons • New York

May those who are led by compassion

lead us all.

Library of Congress Cataloging-in-Publication Data
Talbott, Hudson. Forging freedom: a true story of heroism during the Holocaust / by Hudson Talbott.   p. cm.   Summary: Chronicles the brave exploits of Jaap Penraat, a young Dutch man, who risked his life during World War II to save the lives of over 400 Jews. 1. Penraat, Jaap. 2. Righteous Gentiles in the Holocaust—Netherlands—Amsterdam—Biography—Juvenile literature. 3. World War, 1939–1945—Jews—Rescue—Netherlands—Amsterdam—Juvenile literature. 4. Holocaust, Jewish (1939–1945)—Netherlands—Amsterdam—Juvenile literature. 5. Amsterdam (Netherlands)—Biography—Juvenile literature. [1. Penraat, Jaap. 2. Righteous Gentiles in the Holocaust. 3. World War, 1939–1945—Jews—Rescue—Netherlands—Amsterdam. 4. Holocaust, Jewish (1939–1945)—Netherlands—Amsterdam.] I. Title. D804.66. .P747 2000   940.53'18'09492352—dc21   99-052551   ISBN 0-399-23434-9
10 9 8 7 6 5 4 3 2 1   First Impression

SHABBAS HELPER

Amsterdam 1930

Jaap Penraat knew how to turn a challenge into an adventure. April had come to Amsterdam, making his route home from the market into a maze of vegetable carts and flower stalls. He had just five minutes to run through the course, holding a pickle in one hand and a bundle of eels in the other. Otherwise, his neighbors would be sitting in the dark. Nothing could stop him now. Except, perhaps, Mrs. Greenberg.

"Jaapy!" called the neighbor lady. "Your poor mother's going hoarse from calling you! It's Friday, you know, and you're coming, right? But be quiet because Ira is having a gallstone and . . . "

Jaap nodded and raced onward. The sun was just sinking behind the rooftops when he ran through the kitchen door.

"Well, it's about time!" said Jaap's mother, taking the eels from him. "Mr. Mandelbaum was just here looking for you. You know they're on the dark side of the building. You'd better do their lights first."

"I always do," said Jaap, catching his breath. "I like Mr. Mandelbaum. He has the best stories. And the best cookies."

For the Jewish families in Jaap's apartment building, the Sabbath

began with the Friday sunset. They honored it by not working, not even flipping a light switch. Since Jaap wasn't Jewish, he could turn on the lights for his neighbors. They paid him in sweets and gave him an important-sounding title. He was their "Shabbas Goy."

The Mandelbaums' table was set and dinner simmering on the stove when Jaap knocked on their door. He knew which lamps they wanted lit and quietly set to his task.

"Do you know why we ask you to turn on our lights, Jaapy?" Mr. Mandelbaum asked, setting a dish of macaroons on the table.

"So you can see where you're going?" Jaap answered.

"Well, yes, in a way, you could say that," said the old man. "We are going where our traditions lead us. Whatever the tradition is, even a little thing like not turning a light switch on the Sabbath, it matters that we follow it. The traditions tell us who we are. Our rabbi always says, 'More than the Jews have kept the Sabbath, the Sabbath has kept the Jews.' Now, do you know why *you* do it?"

"For the cookies?" said Jaap.

The old man chuckled. "You may think you do it for the cookies, but I see something else in you. You're a good soul. You like doing mitzvah*s*."

"What are mitzfers?" asked Jaap.

"A *mitzvah* is a good deed, a kindness. Doing something nice for someone just because it feels like the right thing to do."

He patted the boy's head and offered him the cookies.

"Thank you, Mr. Mandelbaum," said Jaap, heading toward the door. "Same time next week?"

"Sure, Jaapy."

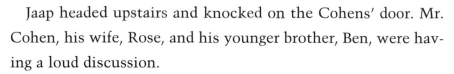

Jaap headed upstairs and knocked on the Cohens' door. Mr. Cohen, his wife, Rose, and his younger brother, Ben, were having a loud discussion.

"These guys must be stopped," said Ben insistently. "They're dangerous!"

"Dangerous?" said Mr. Cohen. "They're in Germany for one thing, and they're a bunch of nuts for another. They'll never get anywhere. The Germans are angry, but they're not stupid."

"What are they angry about?" asked Jaap.

"They lost the big war twelve years ago and their money's still worthless," said Mr. Cohen, "but that doesn't mean they'll turn their country over to a crazy man."

Ben tapped his finger on the newspaper spread on the table. There was a picture of a man in uniform raising his right arm straight out over a crowd raising their right arms toward him.

"They need someone to blame for their own problems," said Ben in disgust. "They need to hurt somebody to feel better about themselves."

"Sort of an *anti*-mitzvah," said Jaap. The Cohens suddenly stopped talking and turned to look at him . . . and then laughed.

"I guess that's a good word for it, Jaapy," said Mr. Cohen. "But this is grown-up talk. You wouldn't understand what we—"

"He knows what a bully is. Don't you, Jaap?" said Ben.

"Enough, Ben!" snapped Mr. Cohen, glaring at his brother. He turned back to Jaap. "You don't have to worry about any of this, Jaapy. It doesn't concern you."

"And probably never will," muttered Ben. Mr. Cohen glared at him again.

"Uh, Jaapy, could you light the dining room first, please?" said Mrs. Cohen. "There's some candied fruit on the buffet, so just help yourself."

Jaap was bothered by the conversation. He brought it up a few days later to his friend Brammy Dorland on their way home from school.

"Bullies—I guess you never get away from them, not even as a grown-up," he said. "I just don't get it. Do you?"

"Well, take Herman, for example," said Brammy. "Actually, just *TAKE HERMAN!*"

The boys laughed. Herman was the school bully. He had gotten left back the previous year, and used his size to terrorize the other kids, especially Brammy. But Jaap and Bram always stood up against the bully together.

When Jaap came to school with his new glasses, Herman tried to grab them. Jaap pushed him away but Herman tripped over his own feet. The crowd on the playground roared with laughter. "All right, Penraat," he said, taking off his jacket, "say your prayers."

They tumbled to the ground, punching and swinging at each other. Suddenly Herman fell backward.

"Brammy!" yelled Jaap. Bram had managed to grab Herman by the collar and yank him off Jaap. Herman seemed glad to have an excuse to quit fighting.

"Don't think I'm finished with you, Penraat," said Herman. "You're gonna get what's coming to you. You and your little Jewboy friend, Dorland. So long, Four Eyes."

Herman and his gang sauntered away, laughing and trading punches. Jaap was a bit dazed. He had never heard the word "Jew" spoken in that tone of voice before. Slowly he rose to his feet and headed home as darkness fell.

FIRESTORM

1933

"These are my treasures. I want you boys to share them," said Mr. Mandelbaum somberly. "Now that you're thirteen, you are old enough."

Jaap and Brammy had been playing chess in the kitchen when the old man entered with two towering stacks of books and set them down on the table.

"They contain ideas," he continued. "They will make you think. That's why they're so afraid of them. They don't want you to think for yourselves. But don't give in to them, boys. No matter who else does. Never give in to them."

There were books on art, music, astronomy, and politics. Einstein, Mark Twain, and Shakespeare were among the names on the worn leather spines.

The old man nodded to Jaap's mother and left.

"Who was he talking about, Mom?" asked Jaap. "Who are *they*?"

"The Nazis," said his mother. "Mr. Mandelbaum is upset about what they did in Berlin last night."

She turned away quickly, hoping that peeling potatoes would mask her own fear. The boys stared at her until she continued.

"The Nazis burned books last night. It was on the radio. They made bonfires out of books written by foreigners and liberals and . . . Jewish people."

Jaap glanced at Brammy. His head was down.

"They could have my math books!" said Jaap, trying to shift the mood. It didn't work.

"I'd better get to my studies," said Bram, putting on his jacket.

"Don't you want to divvy up the books?" asked Jaap.

"Some other time. See you in school. Bye, Mrs. Penraat."

"Will they burn books here, Mom?" Jaap asked after Bram left.

"I can't imagine it," she said quietly. "But people are strange, Jaapy. The worst can be brought out in any of us, under certain circumstances. As well as the best. Be sure you thank Mr. Mandelbaum for the books tomorrow."

Books held a special place in the hearts of the people of Holland. For over four hundred years, the Dutch had been making books in Amsterdam, and Jaap's father, Gerrit Penraat, was part of that tradition. He was a master of a print shop, overseeing the work of fifteen pressmen and printing the finest quality books himself on a special press.

"Jaap, we're going to a meeting tonight," he announced when he came home. "There's a man from Germany who's speaking about—"

"Gerrit, Jaap's too young for that," said Jaap's mother.

"He knows how hard I work to make a book," snapped his father. "I think he needs to know why someone would *burn* one. And I want to know, too."

After dinner the Penraats hurried to the printers' meeting hall. A young couple with two small children sat down next to Jaap.

"Ah! A fellow artist, I see!" said the man, noticing the doodles Jaap had been drawing on his program.

"Well, I'm really better at drawing houses," said Jaap. "I want to be an architect."

"Excellent. But the best architects are truly artists first. My wife, Miriam, is a painter. I write and work a bit with clay when I'm not teaching school. Maybe you'd like to come to our studio sometime and see our work. My name is Eli Cardozo. This is Nathan and the little one is Sam."

The speaker from Germany was a Jewish writer whose work had come under attack. He said the Nazis claimed that any work that did not glorify the German race was anti-German and must be burned. They labeled anyone they didn't like as "enemies of the state." Those who dared speak out were arrested and sent to work camps. The speaker was grateful to be welcomed in Holland, but said they should expect more refugees, for he feared the worst was yet to come.

He was right. The trickle of immigrants from Germany became a flood as conditions worsened in their country. Many refugees escaped with little more than the clothes they wore. The Nazis carted away housefuls of Jewish property, and claimed the empty houses for themselves. For the next five years the madness swept through Germany until it exploded into a rampage of terror on the night of November 9, 1938. Goaded by the Nazis, the Germans burnt down thousands of Jewish homes, businesses and synagogues. There was so much broken glass on the streets afterward that the night came to be known as *Kristallnacht*, the night of the broken crystal.

Jaap and his friends did their best to help settle the refugees crowding into Amsterdam, but the problem was overwhelming.

"We need to help them move on. It's the only way," said Eli at the cafe. "They'll be safer in England or the States."

"Easier said than done," said Jean-Paul, Jaap's friend from Paris. "Nobody has the welcome mat out for Jewish refugees anywhere."

"Holland should just give them Dutch passports," said Miriam.

"Forget it. This government is too scared of offending Hitler," said Carel Blazer, a photographer.

"Speaking of Hitler, look who's coming," said Kreen, Carel's assistant. A large crowd of young men in black shirts and boots came surging through the streets, cheering as if they had won a football game. They were members of the N.S.B., the Dutch Nazi party. Most customers at the cafe moved inside when they saw them coming.

"Over here!" Jaap called out to a young man distributing Nazi pamphlets. "I'll take some and pass them out inside!"

Jaap's friends looked at him in shock.

"Good man!" said the youth. "Say, don't I know you? Penraat, isn't it?"

"Hello, Herman," said Jaap.

"Haven't seen you since school days, back when you used to protect that little Jewboy . . . what's his name? Bramberg? Bramstein?"

"Yeah, well, nice seeing you," said Jaap. "Let me go *distribute*."

"Come to the rally tonight!" said Herman. "To celebrate the Fuehrer's next victory, Poland! Soon, all of . . . hey, what are you doing!"

Jaap tossed the pamphlets into a garbage can. His friends broke into cheers and applause.

"Penraat," muttered Herman. "I should've known you had not changed. You think you're so smart, but we're the ones fighting for our white, Aryan race. Someday you'll thank us. You'll come to appreciate that pamphlet."

"Oh, I feel better already because of it. In fact, it made my day," said Jaap.

"Well, that day is over," said Herman, "and a new one is on the horizon. A new Europe. A new order. You'd better join us. Otherwise, be careful. Amsterdam is a small town."

BLITZKRIEG

May 10, 1940

In the early hours of May 10, 1940, the people of Holland were jolted from their beds by the roar of the Luftwaffe, the German air force, sweeping over the Dutch countryside. German paratroopers moved quickly to surround Holland and cut it off from the rest of Europe. The Germans had now perfected their technique of sudden attack. They called it *Blitzkrieg*—lightning war.

In Amsterdam panic broke out on the streets. People rushed home, desperate to find a safe place when there no longer was one. They huddled by their radios and heard the news that bombs had destroyed Rotterdam. That night the announcement came that the Dutch army had surrendered.

In the Penraats' living room Jaap's family sat motionless for a time.

"What happens now?" asked Jaap's mother quietly.

"Go through the bookcases," said Jaap. "Throw out anything that could get you in trouble. Books by liberals, Jews—"

"So now we're burning our *own* books?" asked Jaap's father.

"We can't take any chances," said Jaap. "And give me that old revolver you had. I'll throw it in the river. A gun is the last thing we want to be caught with."

Two days later, when the Nazis staged their triumphal march through Amsterdam, Jaap noticed the same troops passing him two or three times. They were simply rejoining the end of the parade.

"Of course," he muttered. "You need to scare us so we'll stay in line. Make sure we feel like a bunch of trembling little bunny rabbits, too scared to move. Till you're ready to eat us."

Jaap looked around at his fellow Dutchmen. Bankers, beggars, mothers, and fishmongers all stood alongside each other and wept.

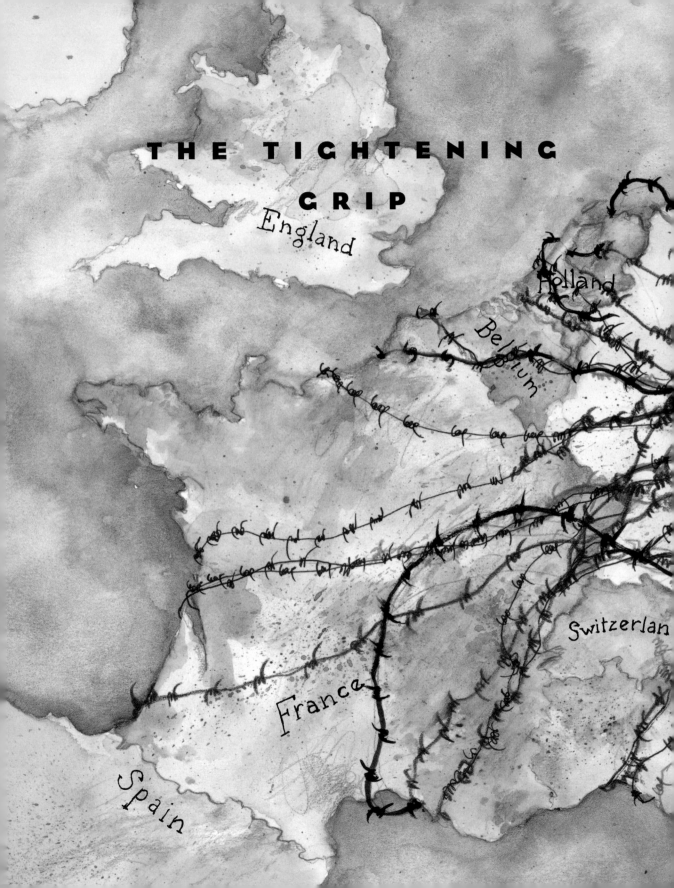

THE TIGHTENING GRIP

England

Holland

Belgium

Switzerlan

France

Spain

By September of 1940 Hitler controlled all of Europe. The Nazis were now free to focus on their next agenda. They began by issuing registration forms to all government employees. Form A was to be filled out by non-Jews and Form B by Jews. Two months later all Jewish employees were fired from jobs in post offices, city halls, and schools, including the one where Eli Cardozo taught.

The Nazis were not making life easy for Jaap, either. He had lost his first job, designing ship interiors, because he refused to join the Nazi architects organization. But still, he knew that he had the choice of joining or not joining. Eli and his other Jewish friends were not so lucky. They spent their days looking for any odd job that they could find, and trying to avoid the Dutch Nazi hoodlums.

Jaap was sitting alone in the cafe late one January afternoon when Eli sat down and threw his new identification card on the table. It looked exactly like the one all Dutch citizens had to carry, with one distinction. On the lower left was stamped a big black J.

"So now they're branding us," said Eli. "So much more convenient when they stop us on the street."

Jaap studied it for a moment. "I have an idea," he said. "Got any bleach?"

Nathan and Sam, now fourteen and eleven, watched the adults set up their work area in the Cardozos' dining room. Jaap tested a tiny drop of bleach on his own card. It removed the ink but left a white blotch.

"Won't you get in trouble for that?" asked Sam, the eleven-year-old.

"Shut up, you idiot," said Nathan, "don't you understand what they're doing?"

"Boys, listen to me," said Eli, taking the shoulders of his two sons. "I don't like having to say this but, right now, you've got to be grown-up. We don't know what's going to happen to us. Jaap wants to help but he's taking a risk just being here. Nothing must go beyond this room. Understood?"

The boys nodded. Meanwhile, Jaap was having no luck with the bleach.

"Lend me the cards," he said finally. "And stay home for now."

He returned the next day and handed Eli his new card.

"What do you think?" he asked. There was neither a J nor a white blotch.

"I think you're a genius," said Eli. "But I don't think I look much like a Hans Van Kampen!"

"You do now. And you, my dear, are starting to look just like a Louise Dorner!" said Jaap, handing a new card to Miriam.

"So where did you get these?" asked Miriam.

"You don't need to know that," said Jaap. "Let's just say Hans and Louise can get new cards and they'll still be as Christian as the day they were born."

"But these are their thumbprints, and their signatures," said Miriam.

"And *your* photo. Look, the Germans are only looking for the J. This will at least get you your food rations. Just don't act suspicious and you'll be fine."

Realizing that all of his Jewish friends' ID cards now needed "fixing," Jaap asked the non-Jewish people he trusted to "lose" their ID cards, which he then "found" and altered. A small operation sprang up in Jaap's bedroom as the "lost" ID cards came in and the "fixed" cards went out. Carel Blazer and Kreen made the new photographs.

Within a month Jaap was forging all kinds of papers. Papers were needed for everything—to own a radio or a telephone, to stay out past curfew, for travel, moving, working, or not working. Compared to the ID cards, the permits and exemption papers were relatively easy to counterfeit. They were usually no more than a mimeograph sheet with a Nazi eagle stamped on them. But a false paper was frequently all that stood between life and death for many Jews.

Tension was filling the city as restrictions around the Jewish community grew harsher. On February 20 the Nazis rounded up 425 Jewish men and sent them to a concentration camp called

Mauthausen. It was more than the people of Amsterdam could bear.

The following morning Jaap discovered the city at a standstill. The shops and stores he passed were closed and there wasn't a streetcar or bus in sight. A crowd was gathering in the main square.

"Isn't it great?" called Eli, running toward him. "Amsterdam is on strike! The railroad employees walked off their jobs about three a.m. protesting the Nazis' roundup yesterday, and then the dockworkers followed them. The action caught on right away, and now the whole city is shut down!"

"What is this?" a Nazi officer shouted from his car at Jaap.

"A strike," Jaap replied.

"Strike? Strike? Impossible! There is no such thing as a strike in the Third Reich!" shouted the startled German as he drove off.

Jaap and Eli laughed, but were amazed themselves. The people of Amsterdam had actually taken back their city from the Third Reich. Non-Jews were risking their lives for the sake of Jews.

The next day two battalions of Nazi stormtroopers drove into town and fired at anyone on the streets. They sent another 300 Jews to Mauthausen and threatened to shoot 500 Jews for each day the strike continued. The strike leaders had no choice but to end it.

At the cafe Jaap's friends debated if the strike did any good. Carel feared even more brutality and Eli regretted the many deaths.

"But look what else happened," said Jaap. "The people who are ready to fight found each other. Our network could be powerful! There's reason for hope."

THE YELLOW STAR

May 1942

For over a year the counterfeit ID cards saved hundreds from arrest, but one morning as Jaap biked into the Jewish quarter to drop off a batch with Eli, he saw that the Nazis had tightened their grip yet again. Sewn onto the jackets and coats of people around them were bright yellow stars, each with a single word written across it—"JEW."

"We had three days to buy them and sew them on," said Eli. "They're even charging us four cents apiece for them!"

"What about yours?" asked Jaap.

Eli shook his head. "I refuse to be a duck in their shooting gallery. Miriam and I have decided to dive underground."

"You're going into hiding? But you have a fake ID."

"That may still work if I'm stopped on the street, but, let's face it, they know where every Jew in Holland lives. It's just a matter of time before they come to get us and I don't want to be there when they do."

Jaap looked around again. "Then why are *they* wearing them?"

"Because they're afraid not to. They're 'law-abiding citizens' just hoping that if they go along with it, they won't get hurt. They just want to do the right thing. I do, too. But what is it, Jaap? What *is* the right thing?"

"I guess whatever it takes to survive, Eli," said Jaap.

By the summer of 1942 the Nazis had enclosed the Jewish quarter with barbed wire and were herding Jews from all over Holland there.

On July 14 they issued an order demanding 4,000 Jewish "volunteers" for slave labor in Germany. No one in Holland was yet aware that any Jew sent to Germany would never return.

The order caused a desperate scramble for hiding places. But hiding in the city was difficult. Neighbors couldn't be trusted, and food was always a problem. Many non-Jewish undergrounders needed hiding places as well.

Jaap devised a good "cover" with a small business he set up making plaster statues of Jesus and Mary. It seemed like a safe haven, during the day at least, for his Jewish employees and his underground circle.

One evening after Kreen had left, Jaap heard the front door open. Two strangers walked into his office.

"Jaap Penraat," said one. "Police. You're wanted for questioning."

On the way to the station Jaap remembered the false ID cards in his wallet. The streetcar was jammed with all ranks of police and Gestapo, secret police. If they found the cards, he could be dead by midnight. Slowly he slipped his hand into his coat pocket.

"Keep your hands where we can see them," said one of the cops.

He cupped his wallet in his hand and held it casually to his side. Their stop was the next one. As the streetcar rounded a turn, the cops moved toward the exit and Jaap dropped the wallet out the window.

"What are you doing?" said a cop, yanking Jaap by the shoulder. "Let's go."

(left) Two editions of *The Jewish Weekly*, stating the latest orders of the German authorities: All Jews not reporting for labor service, moving without permission, or found not wearing the Jewish Star will be sent to concentration camps.

JAIL

August 1942

False papers? What false papers? I have a shop where we make religious statues. Are you sure you have the right name?" said Jaap. He sat in the center of a room surrounded by men from the Bureau of Jewish Affairs.

"Don't bother playing dumb," said an agent. "We know you're involved in a counterfeiting ring. If you give us some names, we'll let you go home."

They grilled Jaap through the night but failed to make him change his story. After three weeks of frustration the Dutch transferred him to the Germans.

For most prisoners the jail of the German Security Police was the last stop before the train ride to Mauthausen, the concentration camp for "enemies of the state." Jaap shared his closet-size cell with three others. The only light came from a hole in the door. A guard passed four slices of bread through it in the morning and a bowl of watery soup at night. A bucket in the corner was the toilet and they slept on the floor.

Jaap discovered a friend in the next cell. Isaac the sculptor was also part of Jaap's underground ring. They communicated through a

hole next to a pipe in the wall. Isaac felt his time was running out. One day he had a request for Jaap.

"It's about my son, Max," he whispered through the wall. "He just turned thirteen. I want him to live, Jaap. Would you take care of him?"

"Isaac, I doubt any of us will get out of here," said Jaap.

"You might. I won't. He's staying with my sister. Please."

The next day guards came for Jaap and led him to the "interrogation hall." For more than three hours the Nazis beat and slapped him, trying to break his will. But they couldn't get any further information out of him. Finally they threw him into a "standing cell," a narrow box with just enough room to stand.

Hours passed until finally the door opened.

"*Komm!*" said a guard, pointing a gun. He led Jaap through a maze of halls and finally opened a huge wooden door to a blinding flood of sunlight.

"*Raus!*" the guard shouted, shoving Jaap out onto the cobblestones. The door slammed behind him. He rubbed his eyes and hoped he wasn't dreaming. After two months in the enemy's hands he was suddenly free again.

A NEW PLAN

Jaap, it's gotten worse since you've been gone," said Kreen.

"I didn't think that was possible," Jaap replied from his bed. He was still recovering from prison.

"It feels like a sinking ship," Kreen continued. "Everybody's trying to cling to the end of the boat that's still sticking out of the water but it's going down fast. The Nazis are taking everybody now. Five thousand, in one night last week! Five thousand in one night! It was awful, Jaap.

"They were going house to house in my parents' neighborhood. We were out in the street in pajamas but there was nothing any of us could do. My dad tried to stop them from taking our neighbor Mr. Meltzer, but he got the butt of a rifle in his face. My mother put her coat around an old lady and they yanked it off. They even emptied out the Jewish nursing home at the end of the street. What could they do with a bunch of old people? It's total madness."

Kreen peered out the window. A Jewish family was being loaded into a truck while the Nazis lit cigarettes and laughed. Kreen shook his head and turned away.

"We can't hide a hundred thousand people. We're lucky if we can

hide *ourselves*. But what are we supposed to do? Just stand here and watch it happen?"

"I've been working on a new idea," Jaap said. "I heard about an underground group working with the Allies. They rescue downed British and American pilots and bring them to France. The French Underground takes them across the Pyrenees to Spain and then the Spanish get them down to Gibraltar, where they pick up a boat to England. Maybe we could set up our own line to get Jews out of here."

"How?" inquired Kreen.

"With false papers. Like the ones we've been making, just a different kind," said Jaap. "I think I can get my hands on documents from a German construction company. I'll copy their letterhead and print it on blank paper so it looks very official, but then I'll write a letter on it saying that the company has hired us to bring workers to their job site in France. Then we use the letter to apply for an official travel permit."

"And this job site would be . . . ?"

"The Atlantic Wall! The Germans are building a huge wall along the coast of Europe, all the way from Norway down to Spain!"

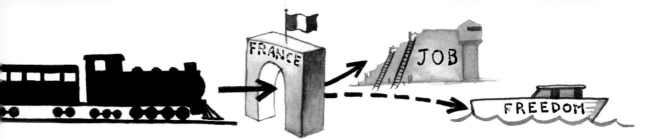

"I know about it, but is this company building it?"

"Who knows? I don't even know if they exist anymore. It's just a chance we'll have to take. But the Nazis have over five hundred thousand people working on the wall right now. They want to make Europe into a gigantic fortress. There's no way they can keep track of who's doing what and where!"

Kreen stood up. He paced back and forth, then stopped suddenly.

"Why don't you just forge a travel permit?"

"I don't have a real one to copy," said Jaap. "Fake papers only work if they're identical to real ones. If it's wrong, we're dead."

"Hmm. That's a problem," said Kreen. "The important permits are issued only in Paris."

Now Jaap was out of bed, also pacing back and forth. "So . . . since we don't have a travel permit yet, we'll have to *sneak* to Paris to get it, right?"

"I think so," said Kreen. "But one more thing. This all depends on having a good connection at the other end. Who do we know in Paris?"

"Jean-Paul! He moved back there at the beginning of the war," said Jaap.

"Of course," said Kreen. "He'll have contacts in the French Underground."

"I'd better get dressed," said Jaap. "We have work to do."

The next day Jaap visited an architect friend who had worked with the German construction company. He gave Jaap a few papers printed with the company logo. That night Jaap set to work transferring the logo to blank paper, using a small press and printer's inks in his father's print shop. The letter had to be written in perfect German, so he asked the help of a German friend who had fled the Nazi regime. With the false signature of the company director, the document was complete.

Jaap blew on it to dry the ink and then laid it down in the center of the table. They stared at it for a long moment, and then looked at each other.

"Well, there's Step One," said Jaap. "And now for Step Two."

"Right," answered Kreen. "Paris."

PARIS

Jaap and Kreen were silent all the way to Maastricht. There were just a few Nazis on board the little train they were now taking to the south end of Holland, but they were thinking about the next one. Since traveling to Paris without papers meant risking their lives in any case, they had decided that their best chance would be to hide in plain sight, riding among the Germans themselves. A German troop train would have no conductors, tickets, or border checks. There was one heading to France that made a stop in Maastricht at midnight. They planned to board it and do their best to blend into the crowd.

The blue-gray dusk of the wintry afternoon had already settled over the medieval town when they stepped off the train. Nightfall in Maastricht, like all of Europe, was unbroken by a single light that could attract the Allied bombers. The two young men wandered the cobbled streets until curfew time, 8:00 p.m. They took refuge in the men's room at the train station and waited.

Shortly after midnight a whistle pierced the stillness. With the screech of brakes the station suddenly filled with German clatter. Jaap and Kreen quickly adopted the frantic mood, and pushed their way up the steps of the train. The car they entered was packed with a full array of the German military.

As the train lurched forward, Jaap and Kreen swayed with the masses of Nazis pressing against them. Luftwaffe, S.S., Gestapo, Security Police, and every rank of the Wehrmacht were all in the mix of uniforms. But there were also many in plain clothes, giving the cover for Jaap and Kreen's own lack of uniforms.

During the night the train slowed and stopped repeatedly as soldiers ran out and checked for bombs hidden under the tracks.

"How ironic," Jaap thought. "Our biggest danger right now is from our own boys in the Belgian Underground."

Nine hours later, Jaap and Kreen emerged at the station in Lille, in northern France. They found their way to a bus heading for Paris. Within a few hours they were standing in Jean-Paul's apartment, gazing out at the Eiffel Tower while he prepared dinner for them.

Jaap and Kreen were awake before dawn the next morning. The day had arrived when they would walk into the lions' den, the Nazi head office called the *Pruefstelle*. Whether they walked out again, with or without the papers, rested entirely on something that old Mr. Mandelbaum called *chutzpah*, his word for "guts."

The Pruefstelle was on the Champs Elysees, the main street of Paris. It was the central clearing office for all permits and licenses in western Europe under the Third Reich.

They decided to wait till noon before entering the Pruefstelle. Fewer people would be around and those who were might be more focused on lunch than on their jobs. If someone called the director of the construction company in Germany to verify Jaap and Kreen's letter, perhaps he would be at lunch, too. Jaap and Kreen knew there were a thousand things that could go wrong. All they could do was to try and minimize them. And hope for the best.

Jaap and Kreen entered the vast marble hall. It was crowded with officials and military personnel. They found the shortest line.

"Good day, miss," Jaap said to the young uniformed woman behind the counter. "I think you'll find our papers in order. We're here to obtain a—"

"One moment, please," she said with her head down, looking at their letter. She filled out a form and paper-clipped it to the letter, then set it aside. "Your travel papers, please."

"But that's what we are requesting," Jaap said evenly. "Ours, as well as the group of workers we will be leading."

The woman looked at him for a moment.

"Yes, of course," she finally said. "Please return to this window between three and four p.m."

"Will you still be here?" asked Jaap.

She nodded. Jaap and Kreen tipped their hats and walked away. They both breathed deeply when they were outside again.

"Why did you ask if she would still be there?" asked Kreen.

"To keep it simple," Jaap answered. "Re-explaining our request to another person only doubles the chances for something to go wrong."

"But she asked for our travel papers," said Kreen. "She must've been wondering how we got down here from Amsterdam without them."

"I think I put her off for the moment, but she may figure it out," said Jaap. "We'll just have to wait and see."

"They may be calling that construction company in Germany right now," said Kreen.

"If that's the case, we might as well go and have one last good meal," said Jaap. "We are in Paris, after all."

As they finished dessert, Jaap said, "I think we should go separately to pick up our papers. That way they'll get only one of us. If I'm not out in half an hour, then you'll know something went wrong. Don't stay around here. They'll be looking for you. Go to Jean-Paul and—"

"No, Jaap," said Kreen. "It's better that I go in first. If our plan fails, you're still needed to forge the cards."

They walked down the Champs Elysees until they found an outdoor cafe across from the Pruefstelle. Jaap took a seat and ordered a coffee. Kreen crossed the street and went through the revolving doors.

Jaap tried to remember how long they had waited in line the first time. He closed his eyes and wondered about his judgment. Why didn't he go first? What had he gotten his friend into? What were they thinking . . . that they could pull a "fast one" on the Third Reich? That they could fool the Nazis?

"Jaap, wake up. We did it," said Kreen quietly.

The newly issued travel permit was lying on the table in front of him. There were also blank documents for the twenty "workers" they would be leading.

"Well, I guess that wasn't our last meal after all," said Jaap.

"Guess not," said Kreen. "Let's celebrate with dinner!"

FINAL TOUCHES

S o the first question is: Who do we take?" stated Kreen as they unlocked their bicycles outside of Amsterdam's Central Station.

"We'll start with friends," said Jaap. "People we trust, in the gravest danger, who fit the type. That means no women, no men over thirty-five, and no kids. It's lousy, but it's the only way it'll work. They have to pass as construction workers."

"That still leaves lots of people. We only have twenty forms."

"And that's all we're taking. If this thing works, it'll be a miracle," said Jaap. "But I was still thinking I should try to copy the form. No sense writing on the originals. My dad could help me with making copies. Meanwhile, we have to start putting the word out."

The next night, Jaap met his father at the printshop. They waited until the other pressmen had gone home and then set to work etching a plate made from the original Nazi form. Then they ran off several copies on a small press. Jaap took them home and added the bold red stripes by hand using a straight edge. The final touch was the eagle and swastika stamp.

Jaap heard a noise outside his door. He threw a blanket over his setup, and held perfectly still.

"Jaap, it's Eli."

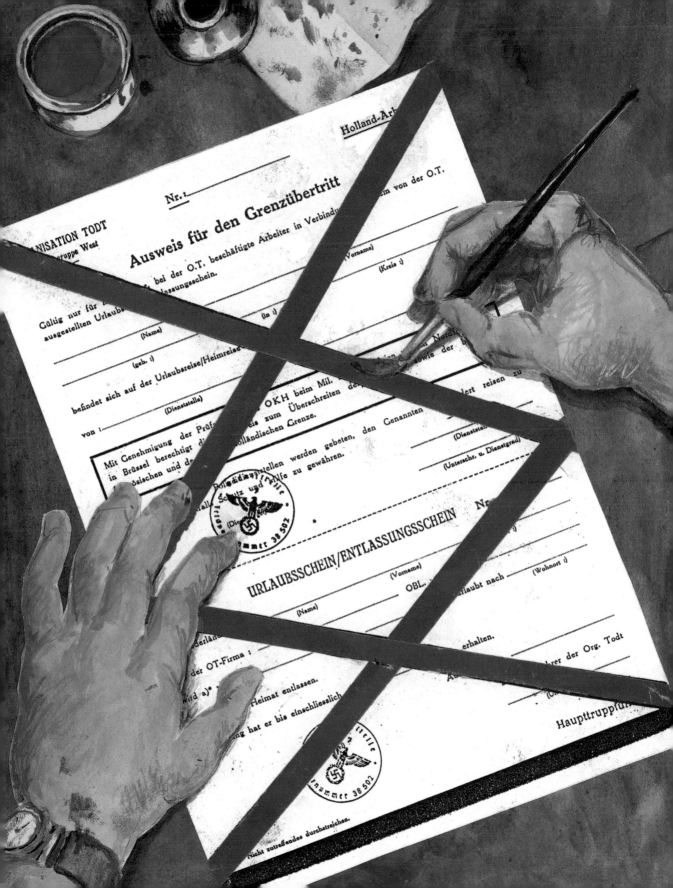

"Eli!" said Jaap, quickly letting in his friend and shutting the door. "It's past curfew!"

"Jaap, take my boys," said Eli. "It's their only hope."

"You heard about the plan already?" asked Jaap.

"It's a pretty short grapevine."

Jaap paced around the room. How could he say no to Eli? Yet, they were children. It was impossible.

"Eli, we'll take you. Let the boys stay here with their mother till we figure something else out."

"Jaap, you know I would never leave Miriam alone," said Eli. "Look, I've had a life. The boys deserve one, too. I know they can do it. Please. Come see for yourself."

Jaap took out a false post-curfew permit, and two permits for bicycles. They biked over to the Cardozos' hiding place, in the cellar of a friend's house.

Miriam was putting the finishing touches on Nathan and Sam. They were now sixteen and thirteen, and both had grown several inches since the last time Jaap had seen them. They wore bulky sweaters to fill out their overcoats. Their black curly hair was cut short and floppy-brimmed hats shadowed their young faces. Wire-rimmed glasses added a few more years. They had also smudged their chins with a little burnt cork to give the effect of a beard.

"What do you think?" asked Sam.

Jaap hadn't thought about this aspect of the plan. Was he now the one who passed judgment on who stays, who goes? Who lives, who dies? The family stood silently watching him.

"I think," he began slowly, "that you'd better let me do the talking when they check papers."

The boys nodded. Eli and Miriam hugged Jaap, but it was hard for any of them to muster a smile.

For the next two weeks Jaap and Kreen organized their group. Ben Cohen, Jaap's neighbor, was one of the first. Jaap tracked down Max, the son of his friend from prison, Isaac. He was just fourteen but a stocky, athletic type. With the right photo for his new ID, he could pass for seventeen.

One evening Jaap stopped by his father's shop after receiving a message from him. Someone was waiting to see him.

"Brammy!" exclaimed Jaap, throwing his arms around his old friend.

"Hi, Jaap! It's been a long time. And it's Bram now!" he said with a smile.

"Where have you been? I haven't seen you since you left for rabbinical school."

"We were living with my uncle in a village near Utrecht since the beginning of the war. But then they brought all the Jews back here last week and stuck us in the ghetto. I had to sneak out since I don't have a permit to be on the street. Your father told me about your plan. Jaap, I want to go with you. Will you take me?"

"You don't need to ask, Bram," said Jaap. "You're partly the reason I'm doing it. You would do it for me. Who knows if it will even work, but it seems like the best chance we have for now. Can you get any workman's clothes?"

"I'll find something, but I can't be on the streets," said Bram.

"I'll make you a new ID. My friend Kreen can photograph you tonight," said Jaap. "It's important for you to come to a meeting tomorrow. We'll go over the plan and you'll meet the others."

PACK AND PRAY

December 1942

The next afternoon a small group gathered in a friend's apartment. They came dressed in what they were planning to wear. Most of the outfits passed inspection but anything too fancy or bright was thrown out. A few had tried bleaching their hair to appear more "north European" but, with dark beards shadowing their faces by five o'clock, it looked fake. They decided that crew cuts and caps were the better solution.

Jaap made sure that everyone had a new non-Jewish ID card, and then filled out the corresponding travel papers. They had different identities now and needed to be ready to answer any questions about their new lives. Jaap's most important task was to convince them to let go of their fear. They were no longer students, teachers, artists, or musicians, but construction workers on their way to a job.

"What happens when we get to France?" asked Nathan.

"We'll be meeting a man named Henri on the platform in Lille. He's a friend of a good friend of mine. You can trust him. He'll take you to a 'safe house.' Then you'll go into the underground 'pipeline' till you reach Spain."

"We have to crawl through a pipeline to Spain?" asked Sam.

"No, no. That's just an expression," said Jaap. "It's actually a network of people who are going to take care of you. They'll take you from one safe house to the next till you get to Spain. From there the Spanish Underground will take you to Portugal, and in Portugal you'll get on a boat to England. The English have a big center for Jewish refugees. You'll stay there till the war's over and—"

"And we can see our parents again," added Sam.

"Right," said Jaap. "For the rest of you, Henri can arrange for your passage to Spain also, but you'll be free to go your own way if you prefer. It will be up to you. Any other questions?"

"What can we bring with us?" asked Max.

"As little as possible," said Jaap. "You're going to be on the road for a long time. Bring some food for the trip. And a joke or two. Laughter is the best camouflage for nerves."

"So . . . where and when, Jaap?" asked Bram.

"We'll meet just inside the main door of Central Station tomorrow night at exactly 8:45," said Jaap. "The train leaves at 9. I'll have your tickets. If you see me talking to a cop or a German, don't come near. Just stay calm and keep walking. Look for Kreen if you don't see me. And remember your chutzpah."

The young travelers needed that reminder as they reflected on why they were taking this risk. Certainly the chance at a future for themselves was important, but something deeper was driving them. They were the hope of their families and community. Hiding passively while Hitler destroyed their culture had become unbearable. Many were heading to England to join the British Armed Forces, the only European force left fighting the Nazis. They spent their last day saying good-bye to their old lives and preparing for the new ones.

Jaap was also preparing himself. He chose a heavy coat like the ones worn by German soldiers in the north. In the mirror he watched himself walk with confidence and speak with authority. He had to believe he was the *Transport Fuehrer*, or transport leader, if the scheme was to work at all.

His last stop before the station was the Cardozo household. The boys stood still as Eli tucked their wool scarves around them and Miriam packed food containers into their duffel bags. At last there was nothing left to do. Jaap hugged the parents and then went out to the street, giving the family their last moments alone together.

A few minutes later Nathan and Sam emerged from their hiding place, pale and red-eyed. Sam was muttering something in Hebrew.

"It's a prayer he was learning for his Bar Mitzvah," said Nathan.

Jaap waited until he was finished. "From now on our prayers must be silent," he said gently. The boys nodded.

THE JOURNEY

At 8:40 Kreen appeared by the door of Central Station. Then Jaap arrived with the Cardozo boys. From different parts of the station the young men slowly gathered at the meeting place. At 8:50 Jaap took a head count. Everyone was there. He passed out the tickets and led the group toward their platform.

Jaap noticed that they stood out more than he had anticipated. There were no other large groups of passengers in plain clothes.

"Halt!" shouted a German security policeman from a distance. He motioned for Jaap to come toward him. The group stopped in their tracks.

"Papers, please," he said in German. Jaap produced his ID card, travel permit, and the all-important permit for transporting labor groups. The German studied them. "You're the first leader of this type that I've seen here. They are so hard up for men in France?"

"I think so, sir," said Jaap confidently. "They are adding on more and more as the project grows."

"Very well," he said, handing Jaap's papers back to him. "I suppose I'll be seeing more of you here, then."

"Most likely. Good day," said Jaap, turning away.

"Just a minute," said another voice. A Dutch cop came forward. "You're Penraat, aren't you?"

Jaap nodded. He held out his papers.

"Sergeant Klempner. Sergeant *Herman* Klempner," he said.

"Herman," said Jaap. "Small world."

"Small town, anyway. I said that to you years ago, as I recall," he said, looking through Jaap's papers. "What is all this?"

"I've been hired to lead a work crew to their job site in France. I am the *Transport Fuehrer* for Organization Todt."

"Todt is a state-run organization," said Herman. "You're telling me you're now working for the Third Reich?"

"My German colleagues know everything about my past. Obviously I wouldn't have this job if they didn't trust me now. So, if there's nothing further . . . "

"Papers! Let me see their—" The train whistle blew. Jaap signaled for his men to get on board. Then he turned back to Herman.

"Nice to see you again, Klempner," said Jaap, jumping on the steps of the train. "Perhaps we'll see more of each other now that we're on the same team! Auf Wiedersehen!"

"Penraat!" shouted Herman, jogging alongside the departing train. "I've got my eye on you."

Jaap scrambled up the steps and began the search for seats. The car was divided into twelve compartments, each with six seats. They had found seats for almost everyone when a problem erupted.

The last three seats in the entire car were in a compartment already occupied by three Nazi officers. Nathan, Sam, and Max stood by the doorway but the Nazis refused to let them enter.

"This is a private compartment! Out!" the Nazis shouted in German.

"Excuse me, sir, but we are assigned twenty-two seats in this car," said Jaap quickly. "And since all the others are taken . . . "

"Out! No foreigners in here! Can't you see this is an officers' compartment, you idiot!" screamed the angriest German. "Get these urchins out of my sight! We are officers of the Third Reich. You do not want to irritate us."

"Of course not, sir," said Jaap. "But this is not a military train. We have our orders also."

The Nazi's face reddened with fury.

"You have five seconds to leave my sight!" he snarled. "Out!"

Jaap turned to the boys and gestured for them to stand in the corridor. He disappeared and returned several minutes later with a huge Nazi wearing a shiny helmet and a silver breastplate. The *Zugstreife* was the master of the train.

"These are my men, Herr Commandant," said Jaap. The train master checked their tickets and papers. "They have important work to do," Jaap continued. "Completing the Atlantic Wall is a top priority! No one knows where or when the enemy will invade. The future of the Third Reich may depend on their work."

The train master stepped into the compartment with the other Germans. Their exchange began politely, but as it grew more heated, he slid the door shut. Suddenly, it slid open again and the most irate Nazi stood in the doorway, glaring at Jaap. He flicked his cigarette ashes, then turned and strode down the corridor, followed by his two cronies. The train master then gestured toward the empty seats, and left.

"I guess we had the bigger Nazi," whispered Jaap.

The three boys cautiously sat down in the seats where the Nazis had been, then looked at each other and laughed. "Rabbi Schulman would be so proud," said Max.

For the next few hours the boys rehearsed details of their new "lives." Jaap had coached them to keep their stories simple. Ben Cohen, who was now "Hans Bakker," planned to say he was a bricklayer. Nathan, Sam, and Max would say they were orphans old enough to make their own way in the world. No one knew what would be asked but they were certain their lives depended on their answers.

The train came to a halt at the Belgian border. Every passenger was required to step off and join a line filing into the customs office. Jaap and Kreen gathered their men into a single file behind them and waited their turn.

Passing between the armed guards Jaap entered the office alone and presented his papers to the customs officers. They had not heard of anyone called a *Transport Fuehrer* and took some time inspecting the document. Jaap tried not to think of what would happen if they rejected his papers. There was no Plan B. No escape route from this point. He pictured the customs officer getting a medal for catching them.

When he heard the sound of a rubber stamp hitting his paper, Jaap quietly exhaled. The boys filed through the office as Jaap and Kreen stood nearby, enjoying the repeated thump of the stamp hitting the twenty false transit papers. Back on board, the boys stared at the new stamp marks, barely believing what they had just done. The train was now in Belgium.

Before reaching Brussels the train slowed down near a bridge.

"Another checkpoint?" asked Sam.

"I don't think so," Jaap said. "They're looking for land mines or loosened bolts. The Belgian Underground does its job well. Most of the train sabotage is done by former railroad men."

"How do the Germans know when they've found all the bombs?" asked the boy.

"The train doesn't blow up," said Jaap.

Sam was quiet after that.

At approximately 3:00 a.m. they arrived in Brussels. Germans came through the train, checking papers again. Jaap looked around at his sleepy crew and feared that this would be the time when someone would make a slip. The Nazis glanced at a few papers but then left them alone. As soon as the train pulled away from the station, the boys were whispering again. The sleep was as false as their ID cards. They're catching on, Jaap thought.

The train slowed several more times as it was crossing the plains of Flanders. The boys were becoming used to it when shots rang out in the distance, and then shouting in German. Everyone in Jaap's compartment sat up and looked at each other.

"They must've found one!" exclaimed Sam, looking to Jaap.

"That's not a bomb, that's gunfire!" said Jaap.

The roar of a British Spitfire overhead swept down the length of the train, punctuated by the repeating blasts of machine-gun fire.

"Get on the floor!" shouted Jaap. "Away from the windows!" He crawled out the door and yelled down the corridor, "Everybody down!"

Another line of the plane's machine-gun fire hammered down the train. Suddenly, the train jolted violently.

"We've been hit!" cried Sam.

"I don't think so," said Jaap. "The Germans are firing back. They have anti-aircraft guns mounted on flatbed cars."

Another plane passed overhead, strafing gunfire from the back to the front of the train this time. The return blasts from the Nazi cannons bounced the train from both ends. Searchlights streaked out across the sky now from the flatbeds, hunting for the R.A.F. fighter planes.

"Those are my guys up there!" said Solomon, a headstrong nineteen-year-old. "Hey, Jaap, I'll tell 'em to lay off the trains from Amsterdam to Lille. Soon as I join!"

The British pilots managed to dodge the lights and still sweep in for a cross attack. Window glass shattered through the car. German soldiers ran down the corridor on their way to replace those who had been hit on the flatbed car. More blasts from the rear cannon jarred the train.

This time the Germans scored a hit. A plane spiraled downward into a explosion of flames in a nearby field. Through a machine-gun bullet hole Jaap watched the pilot's parachute open, silhouetted against the firelit sky.

The cannon jolted the train a few more times but the planes' buzz faded in the distance. Slowly, Jaap and the others straightened up and brushed the bits of glass and debris off themselves. It was now close to dawn.

The Belgian-French customs office was barely distinguishable in the fog as the battered train came to a halt. The officers on duty were curious about Jaap and Kreen's unique work order but as soon as they saw the stamp from the first border crossing, they added their own. With the last papers stamped Jaap and his group returned to their seats and the train entered France.

A few of the younger boys were growing energized by the prospect of stepping out into a foreign country. But Jaap was focused on what lay ahead. The upcoming moment of transfer on the platform was the most dangerous one. The Germans had many double agents planted in the underground. The "Henri" that Jean-Paul knew could have long since been caught and replaced by a pro-Nazi Henri, and no one would know that until it was too late.

The station's cavernous gray structure rose above a sea of tracks. Men in berets pushed carts of luggage. German Security Police strolled the platforms, along with many S.S. officers. There were dozens of strangers who could be Henri.

Jaap and Kreen led the group onto the busy platform.

"I think he's going to have to find us," Jaap whispered to Kreen.

"That guy in the black overcoat is watching us," said Kreen. "What do you think?"

"I'll pass by and see what happens," said Jaap. "Get the boys off the platform if I stay away too long."

Jaap walked by the man. He stopped a few feet away and fiddled with his watch. The stranger approached.

"You are Jacques?" he said quietly. "I am Henri. Jean-Paul told me you like duck with orange sauce. You had it with him in Paris two weeks ago."

"Jaap is the name," he said, holding out his hand. "But you can call me Jacques."

They walked back to the group. The platform was clearing now and they needed to move away to avoid any attention.

"Henri, these are the guys," said Jaap. "Men, I guess this is it. Maybe we'll see each other back in Amsterdam someday. Good luck in your new lives, but don't forget you're Dutchmen."

He shook each man's hand quickly until he reached Nathan and Sam.

"I'll tell your parents you did great," he whispered.

"I hope we can be friends when I get back to Amsterdam, Jaap," said Sam. "I'm about the age you were when you met my dad."

"I know, Sam," said Jaap. "And, sure, we'll always be friends. Like me and Bram. Right, Bram?"

"Right, Jaap," said Bram, the last one to shake Jaap's hand.

Jaap smiled at his friend. "I guess there's nothing left to say except *L'chaim!*" Jaap whispered. "To life."

"*L'chaim*, Jaap," said Bram softly. "To life."

After a moment, Henri moved forward. "They will be safe soon, Jacques," he said quietly, "but we must go now."

Jaap and Kreen watched the boys walk through the train station and out the front door.

"They're free, Jaap," said Kreen. "The plan worked."

"It'll work even better next time," said Jaap.

"Next time?"

"I'm a counterfeiter, remember? Let's see if we can copy it!"

4 0 6   L I V E S

Within three weeks Jaap led another group of disguised Jewish youths to France, and Kreen led the next one. As their system improved, they made trips more frequently, for there was not a moment to spare. In the opposite direction the Germans were sending trainloads of Jews to their deaths in concentration camps. By the middle of 1943 the Nazi plan to exterminate all Jews was in full gear, and they were no longer bothering to hide it.

The tide of the war, however, was turning against the Germans. A massive Allied invasion would bring an end to the Atlantic Wall scheme. The Allied bombers were already targeting almost anything that moved on the ground, making Jaap's trips increasingly dangerous. By late May of 1944, as his train rolled slowly through another bombed out station, Jaap felt that he had pushed his luck as far as he could. With the great showdown between the Allies and the Axis about to occur, he decided to cease his missions. He had made over twenty trips and rescued a total of 406 people from the Nazi death camps. A week later, on June 6, 1944, the Allied Forces landed in Normandy. All of western Europe became a battlefield.

In Holland, the Nazis sent any remaining food back to Germany and enslaved all able-bodied Dutchmen as laborers for their crumbling war machine. Jaap fled to the countryside with three friends.

They hid in a barn through the darkest time of the war, the Hunger Winter of 1944–1945. Over 2,000 people per week died of starvation.

The Jewish ghetto was now empty, for the Germans had completed their deadly mission. Any Jews still in hiding depended on outside help for survival. Jaap slipped into Amsterdam once a week with food for friends in need.

By spring, word was spreading that the Allies were close. Jaap was biking through town one day when the sound of cheering drew him toward the main square. People were running out of their houses waving the national colors. Down the street, the tanks of the Canadian First Army Corps were just coming into view. A young soldier popped out of a hatch, waving a tiny Dutch flag.

Jaap closed his eyes and drifted for a moment. It had been so long since he had heard laughter. He pictured Eli and Miriam running along with Nathan and Sam, and Brammy waving to him. He thought about all of his friends and neighbors who had vanished long ago. He remembered old Mr. Mandelbaum.

"We won, Mr. Mandelbaum!" Jaap imagined saying to his friend. "The war is over! Amsterdam is ours again!"

The old man smiled, but didn't seem concerned. "You see what I told you, Jaapy," he said. "You like doing mitzvahs. That was a mitzvah."

"It's what we're supposed to do, isn't it, Mr. Mandelbaum?" whispered Jaap. He looked out at the people of Amsterdam. "I just did what I could."

Jaap Penraat, 1943

Author's Note

I happened to have the radio on one afternoon when I heard Jaap Penraat being interviewed about his wartime activities. Jaap and I had already been friends for over twelve years, but for all the holidays, birthdays, and pleasant evenings we had spent together I had never heard a word about his heroic past. When I called him the next morning to inquire about his story he seemed surprised and honored that I would even take an interest in it.

But I am far from alone in recognizing the significance of his work. In 1974 the Dutch government awarded him a war pension, and in 1981 honored him again with the *Verzetsherdenkingkruis*, the Cross of the Resistance. On June 11, 1998, I was happy to be present at an award ceremony for Jaap at the Israeli Consulate in New York. The award certificate, read by the consul General, stated:

"This is to certify that, in its session, the Commissioner for the Designation of the Righteous, established by Yad Vashem, the Holocaust Heroes and Martyrs' Remembrance Authority, on the basis of the evidence presented before it, has decided to honor Jaap Penraat, who, during the Holocaust period in Europe, risked his life to save persecuted Jews. The commission, therefore, has accorded him the medal of the Righteous Among the Nations. His name shall be forever engraved on the Honor Wall in the Garden of the Righteous, at Yad Vashem, Jerusalem."

On the medal is inscribed an ancient Proverb:

"He who saves a single human life saves the entire universe."

H.T.